In the archives

In the archives

Christopher Arigo

OMNIDAWN
RICHMOND, CALIFORNIA
2007

Cover art: Christopher Arigo, In the archives (2), 2004, collage on board; 8″ x 8″.

Book cover and interior design by Ken Keegan

Offset printed in the United States on archival, acid-free recycled paper by Thomson-Shore, Inc., Dexter, Michigan

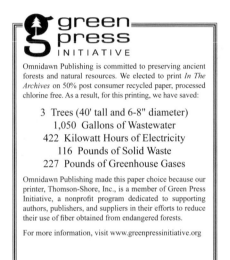

Omnidawn Publishing is committed to preserving ancient forests and natural resources. We elected to print *In The Archives* on 50% post consumer recycled paper, processed chlorine free. As a result, for this printing, we have saved:

3 Trees (40' tall and 6-8" diameter)
1,050 Gallons of Wastewater
422 Kilowatt Hours of Electricity
116 Pounds of Solid Waste
227 Pounds of Greenhouse Gases

Omnidawn Publishing made this paper choice because our printer, Thomson-Shore, Inc., is a member of Green Press Initiative, a nonprofit program dedicated to supporting authors, publishers, and suppliers in their efforts to reduce their use of fiber obtained from endangered forests.

For more information, visit www.greenpressinitiative.org

Library of Congress Catalog-in-Publication Data

Arigo, Christopher.
    In the archives / Christopher Arigo.
        p. cm.
    Poems.
    ISBN 978-1-890650-31-5 (pbk. : acid-free paper)
    I. Title
    PS3601.R54I6 2007
    811'.6--dc22

                        2006102755

Published by Omnidawn Publishing
Richmond, California
www.omnidawn.com   (510) 237-5472   (800) 792-4957
        10 9 8 7 6 5 4 3 2 1

ISBN: 978-1-890650-31-5

In memory of Beulah and Rosario Arigo
— who realized first

Contents

Abbreviated inventories

Abbreviated inventories I

(A) Is this war

is this a slow burn / are these rotor-blades that savage

the air rarefied and a thudding rhythm

a riotous array of tensions ingrained and bodies' imaginary

light strained through winter inversions

—who knew sun-spilt sky sustains so little

that helicopters cannot fly unnoticed

that they mutter obscene fricatives / that they must be

and cannot be

still

(B) Tactile experiments are underway

static and whirring

weather asunder—why talk about it

still too warm for a spotlight's intrusion

—a warming sensation that something will end

or recur or will start its scurrilous engine

that any inventory as such only reveals so much

that some thing or some one has alighted

wings angulated around its own body or his / hers / my body—otherwise

not much to report today

(C) And then some one said / and then some one said

the measure of flight is height not distance flown

to go up / to circle the same staggered plane requires aloofness

to navigate—while flight requires more than

faith / that barbules keep feathers fluent / that hollow bones keep bodies slight

that rectrices end the body's inventory and what happens next

in taxonomy will be remembered mnemonically for another decade or so

—what happens next when the temperature fails to rise

above freezing remains undetermined

still

Abbreviated inventories II

(A) Not the present tense of *to tear* / not saline tears either but

repetitive tensiled gestures

curtains shorn from rings

möbius coils

radium sparks fluoresce

shouts clarify the hushing night—

(B) It rains

and sickly-blue water submits to its dendritic course

möbius in its serpentine bends and elbows—

aquatic displacement fills

with fish-dreams and few far-seeing eyes

maps cannot keep up with erosion / with what is carried downriver

(C) Night interrupted by comets and brush-

heated calligraphy—beyond the given curve of earth

\horizon afterglow

whistles of streaking bombs elide into one sustained antiphony of twisted notes

someone forges thunder-teeth from celestial origins

ages of metal and war ushered by streaks of light and celestial geomancy

magma tears airborne and quick-cooled

numinous patina of sweat

knapped fragments fit well in hand—from *innocuous* to *weapon*

impact craters burst and stretch to re-embrace the sky

Abbreviated inventories III

(A) Aftermath is the first concern

will the numbers subtract or subside

surely escape is possible even permissible

lightning frees ions

wheels lock in mud while the sky

is only a painted backdrop / an abstract stretch of space

oriented sundial

soporific decline

symbiont of light

(B) Caught undertongue confessions fall flat

—the liquor of disappearing spittle could intoxicate nations

an astringent breeze unrests the evening

follows lightning

limbs orient with compass needles—hesitant and toddling

eyes in conflict / eyes spin in shifting magnetic fields

uncertain upon which direction to fixate

(C) Right hand weaves a basket with the left—polydactyl warp—

to contain reports abbreviated in scope

steeples shudder with noise appropriate to the hour

legs and arms extend and chests heave

but the head—the head could divulge or explode any second

bells resound despite the hour

explosions underground

hands pressed to forehead to contain the deluge

Abbreviated inventories IV

(A) Unreal language spreads across borders—cold jokes

metallic smells / ozone smells machine-gun the senses

when a festival of cruelty gathers by the river

to swear oaths in a hell-fire dialect

whose malice does not translate

B) Among rushes and horsetails

the barbarians' tremulous shouts

rise / shadows rise purple and withdraw

the festival inhabits their hands and dictates marionettes

whose taut wires cast barely-shadows—and

in this turgid riparian zone

swamps have voices of rot

(C) Omens occlude visible planets

include them shivering light-years away

shimmering staccato spheres

drum-rolls across the valley ratchet the present tense *to fear* / *to terror-*

ize / to set ablaze and stand back / to watch

flames insistent against shadows

against a backdrop of waxen faces and clipped wires

—scarecrows aligned along the riverfront

voodoo river / they do

cicada chirr / the heat lightning

Abbreviated inventories V

(A) Another marshy squabble ends and they gather

to toss wish-pennies / to gaze long and lovingly at their reflections

leaking heat into gelid air—who will feel that

diminished draft when

games end / when songs and lightning suspend

present tenses

(B) Gathered by the river

the festival ends with obsidian knives

lightning sears invisible rivers

—there are invisible planes aloft somewhere

hordes storm melting darkness

—an elaborate horror flick that dries mouths / riverbeds

(C) Thoroughly orchestrated rain

adds atmosphere / thunder adds resonance / recurrences add

cohesion

or the illusion thereof

Breath variations

Breath variations

0.

These scavenged	*[These foundling]*
remnants can-	
not be beyond	*[not transcend]*
human beyond	*[human transcend]*
what that might	
entail—after all	
they breathe	
morning into	*[us into being.]*
being.	[ ]

1.

Your hand
cupping mouth
creates silence—   [*elides silence*]
an entrance—   [*prevents entrance*—]
the gesture
of a reticent   [*of a surprised*]
child or some-
one implying
no more.   [no more.]

2.

What cracked vessels   [--------------------------]
struggle to contain   [--------------------------]
to prevent spilling   [--------------------------]
from your throat: [--------------------------]

--------------------------.

3.

Overlip spills   [*Out of your mouth*]
more than   [*spills more than*]
water more than
stars and satiation
into your awaiting
hand. The breathing   [*ear. The breathing*]
that haunts you
spills from lungs
that cannot   [*that refuse to*]
contain it.

4.

To prevent   [*To ignore*]
variant breath
is not so simple—   [*is to sample death*—]
first a lightheadedness
then a slipping away
then urgent inrush
—because the body
must sustain itself   [*must attend to itself*]
even without
your permission.

5.

Pleasure-shell—   [*Empty shells*—]
the body—filled   [*the lungs—fill*]
with blesséd air
and impulses
uncontainable—
blesséd and sustainable
even without will.   [*despite intentions.*]

6.

When counted
breath is conscious   [*breath is imposed*]
effort—a blink—
metered number-
induced inhalation   [*enforced inhalation*]
through the nose   [*through the mouth*]
iambic exhalation
out of the mouth.   [*out of the nose.*]

7.

Whispers conserve
softer air and
brush palate and lips—
secrets interred   [*secrets escape*]
in fractured pots
—affairs and untruths   [*sacred scrolls*]
hidden interminably
in some desert cave
awaiting plunder.   [*awaiting discovery.*]

8.

Inhumation
teeters end-of-tongue
—better to bury   [—*better to speak*]
that utterance
than to speak it   [*than to bury it*]
to regret it   [*to harbor it*]
life-long—its
half-life even longer.

9.

Gathered-up
breath condenses
into atmosphere and fog   [*into faltering words*]
makes greenery more   [*makes your eyes more*]
vibrant—the rustling
is not wind
but verdant growth   [*but ourselves*]
whispering to us.   [*whispering to ourselves.*]

Translation briefs

Translation briefs

0: The window fan ticks out its code...a message that depends on how fast it spins...you translate a few fragments and find them...amenable to...beginnings...to siren squalls...congested avenues...pedestrians waving orange flags to safely cross streets...and around them cars crash and crash...first: the caterwaul of tires...second: the clench of gut ...the anticipation...the rumpled explosion...a caul of sagging windshield...tires unseized on asphalt...you translate the disposition of objects to collide...words to elide...careful excisions in our stories...

47

1: You confound authorities...with half-true stories...you con with injunctions couched in aphorisms::: *Place a stone in your mouth to stave off thirst. / Hold a stone in hand to ward off threats. / A stone undertongue might prevent misquotes...*but doubtful... songs are distractions...you train mannequins to sing...models of angels with white-taut lips...whose eyes reach and seize... synoptic reports that must include the lost...the waiting...the population below them...whose camouflage is obvious to the red/green color-blind...you are the archives...but their radiance makes everything visible...gives everything motion...

48

2: Your procedures to alleviate silence are suspect...your throat a liminal zone...your brain barely charted...echoes insinuate their way into...our conversations' barely tractable surfaces...but we are not alone...*the files we are certain are extensive*...files about departure zones ...where metal and plastic and concrete meet...where furnaces cough red mites... where so much evidence burns with each cycle...aisle after aisle regresses to a perfect vanishing point...a translation of silence...file upon file upon compendia of nomenclature...some hieratic order to disposal...pseudo-angels observe it all...

49

3: We discovered the archives' authoritarian roots…that the versions you worked through are only a turning away…translations of one morsel into another…records overflow in a gravid deluge…uplifted by the interior glow of an inferior light-source…walls close in…and you know the insect desperation of being trapped in sap…*too much…too much…too much…too many*…first: the love letters arrive…second: you implore…*call me by the names of flowers…les fleurs du mal…which one am I*… files yellow…spill over their respective drawers…full of pressed flowers…ambered fossils…catena…agendas…keys…hyponyms…all in urgent need of collation…

50

4: *Do we have too many questions*...and/or do the answers translate into disappointment anyway...detract from the elation of inquiry...the tongue's rapture of syllables...uplifted end-notes...do the archives themselves self-limit...pieced together from smithereens...the city itself motionless...syncretic...*what good can this do*...can friendship encompass desire...can files sort themselves...flirtation mutates into a kind of friendship...can we cease excessive whispering...time to reticulate...to colligate...to discover sources of the bone trade...*must have*...*must have*...the précis we write must encompass this all...

51

5: Arid land dockets must include tectonic movement...volcanic activity...meteorites...*beginnings*: a speck charged by lightning... then free-floating amino acids livid with libidinous potential...but this is the desert now...replete with flowers...prickly pear and saguaro...*orchidae* mimic mates with licentious orange...sandstone sometimes appears orange to scrub and lizards and a *ue*...in the archives an ossified template records...every urgency-elided syllable...books on the subject occupy miles of rows...we imagine every dream has its own volume...along with every dream is a *ue*...a turning toward...filed between desired and forbidden...compendia of endemic cruelty...between a projectile striking glass...and the resulting cone of percussion: *a little diamond of fear*...

6: Accident reports proceed concurrent with more accidents...the archives' windows lit randomly on all thirteen floors...a Christmas-light spiral of people pigeon-holed and numbered...some formula at work...*what seriatim were our responses behind closed curtains*...stray voyeurs...we wander unoblivious to gather evidence...profligate collections of telescopic photos...indices for guidance...walking our fingers through files ordered and cross-referenced: botanical surveys...teeth-grids filed under joy...smiles paralyze us...collapsing shelves paralyze us...tumult near seduction...near fan blades coughing dust...the night air swarms with contagions...with...

53

7: And/or: more than combs that separate strands into elegant rows…braids overlaid and tapered to less unruly whispers…rib cages / clock-work…and/or more than bead strings to keep count…a ticking abacus makes equations concrete …beads linked like spines / chains / millipedes / pinecones…spoons nestled in a drawer as models of efficiency…and/or the file photos and multiple exegeses of object relations…archive walls sandwiching them…matrices arrayed in toppling columns and rows…cross-referenced…and/or the structural grids of skyscrapers …grinning down on city blocks…lights out…teeth missing…honeycombs in trees…deliquescent branches split and unsplit…movement from artery→vein→capillary…and/or herds and hive behavior… a riotous concert or a formation of jets / geese synergistically dividing air…and/or clusters: from atoms to galaxies…*and/or*…

54

8: *Or what*: a progression of questions unravels from its spool of multiple usages…we the inquisitors already thought answers apparent…tinted windows allow only our reflections…to create a gap between *we* and/or where we should have looked first…before turning away…before the snow-blindness inherent in our search…or the fact that it's our turn to respond…and/or translate…*we are not alone in this*…record-keepers maintain their own depictions…how…when…what…their own anatomical studies…their timelines twisting around corners…we must add this line to their stories: *once upon a time*…we must amend the once-inviolate order…

9: We must add the damp that pervades this place...musty residue of cognition...the archives...the dust we cannot tamp down...volumes of our tentative aubades...records of pulse fluctuations and bite marks...each doorway marked with a cipher...we want to return to the window where we began...but conflict prevents safety there...correspondence of the lost...of lust...accumulates fastest in stylized rituals...*and they lived*...where the map room is dingiest...the most difficult to find...to enter we must sign in triplicate in triplicate in triplicate...and each version barely resembles the last...

Catalogued evidence

Catalogued evidence

0. These are the remains of machines:
stilled engines still tic after shutdown,
intimations noticed in dreams or
the scalding awareness of this world
that forces itself inside—
a hypnotic sonata of puns and palindromes.

No radar on defining the circumference
we inhabit—boundaries we agree to call world.
Late fall leaves weighed down by snow are tragic.
In our chests pressure builds.
Tragedy is a violence of smiles.

1. We resist violence machines, witness
their shrieks and moans:
ohgodohgodohgodohgodohgodohgod.
We will not love them nor bleed for them.
We will not advocate cogs and wheels
nor become them.

What we leave: epigrams, residual puns,
mirthless and stubborn. Why complicate
the archives with addenda and marginalia.
The rooms remain empty and maybe
this is what we mean by faith.

2. Trumpet songs of gods and ghosts in machines
lull our ravaged ears—versions of music,
riddles without answers, ambits riddled with gaps.
What strains within our bodies:
what beasts nose our sternums from the inside—
the sensation of balloons blown taut.

What have we taught the children clutching pins—
who some day want to be real puppets,
who already delight in the wispy threads
growing from their fingertips.
A muddled proposition the soul.
Our machines make kingdoms.

3. Difficult to deny the correspondence
of artifacts and evidence.
A so-called new mythology already plays us
masked against a jittering stage of space
and objects frenetic with secret lives,
electric anima revolting against their given names.

Depressions left in pillows as rough fossils
of corporeal needs. Object permanence
requires faith—a child's handprint
in the sidewalk signed and dated.
Fill me with the space you call your self.
Your kingdom is memory,
the archive's shadowy brother.

4. Cenotaphs imply error, a body located only in memory.
Returning air cleaves a narrower space
than leaving and for once you are wordless
—worldless—longing and inexact.
In the ghost-life the living drift away and
you mistake the draft edging under
an unsealed window for memories.

Once you believed in more than this world
as if you could embrace anything more
as if your arms could open that wide
as if ecstasy could substitute for happiness.

5. These are imperfect catalogues for this world.
I confess: this sybarite loves this world.
But to say this is only about love
is to neglect a multitude of hidden machines.
The vox of uncertainty drives gears
of stop-and-start clock hands and
our hands grip these spaces.

The machine that makes the sun
rise is on the fritz.
And we run and we run like clocks working
like clocks working to remember particulars
via repetition or prayer
which are really the same.

6. This is not the world I requested:
encrypted whispers, the map's legend
articulated in cipher or unlit
proving the world, a city, can fit almost anywhere.
Once the world recognized itself from space
but now the obdurate distance
between each disorients each.

Once sunlight composed arresting mosaics
among tree canopies.
One eye opens to itself in darkly polished glass
and now it is insidious.
Now murmurs and shuffling feet.
Now the machine in our chest emits
an uneven ticking.

7. We are the city a thousand times.
Subways clatter and smell ozonic
and pissy and pass through our chests.
Locked in the ghost-chamber,
an umbra in which nothing grows,
trains clack and rush the stricken landscape.

Clatter lamentation and diesel of desire.
Peel back enough skin and maps are vascular braille.
Tunnels intersect our mouths,
our words lost in the cacophony.
So many moths fly desperately to the backs of our eyes.
So often *never* is an epithet for fear.

8. Your eyes have seen all they can today—
relics inventoried in a counting-sheep manner.
Small slivers of light compose their own
muted opus through blinds and a light
comes on in your neighbor's window.
She is marvelous in her awareness of you.
This sybarite loves this world, this moment of respite.

You settle silt-like into memory's rifts
sensing an unrest that is really your own—
You are happy until doubt becomes
consternation and consternation becomes
a steady buzz in your ears.
A new algebra for imbroglio
emerges from our perplexity.

9. Our eyes adjust to half-light again
and instruments demarcate shadows to prolong
—in memory—their inevitable collapse.
Sibilations and sighs comprise
a chorus for eyes to adapt.
Maybe half-light is enough light
if only to see shades and outlines.
Vision recedes to a camera obscura.

Some lenses enable us to see in the dark
objects eerily green-hazed—
a candle miles away becomes a radiant star
and finally there we are:
role-reversed, a galactic explosion,
ecstatic like never before.

10. Ghostly contrails hesitate to dissipate
long after a plane's passing—
only the pressure of this atmosphere
keeps you—the lyric you and my breath.
Shadows return to your face
from whatever aphotic box contained them.

Footnoted and annotated, a list
guides the mind, the almost excessive
adulation of something awry—
of something nearly paradisiacal
—close to maniacal. The frenetic energy
of your worship wanes with night.

11. Amber is the color of your waking—
mine is a blue-hued cartography
of cranial shadows, moths in a jar among
many jars among dreams. Sleep thins
to mourning doves wooing grief.
Sleep drives out the white spaces
within my body. Only the pressure
of this atmosphere keeps you buoyant.

Open my jars one by one.
Stun me with the space you call your self.
You hang a do not disturb sign
hoping for a moment of respite.
The world while sleeping can be called
temporarily out of order.

12. And what is inside barely fits.
Bodies accrete half-dreams.
One memory nestles inside the next.
But sleep thins to strophic layers,
unregistered marginalia for an incomplete opus,
eidetic visions, pentimenti accumulated
on sketches, doors open to admit
too many jumbled analects.

Pipes bang like prisoners in the wall.
Apertures—your eyes—lustrous wounds
that predictably hurt as they heal.
The air the lost displaces
must be comparable, somehow, to living.
The story must end with living
a dialogue with death that terminates
with laughter, synonymous with oblivion.

13. A thin trickle of water stains the porcelain.
Leaves are blown loose every other day
when a helicopter lands thrice weekly
on the H at the hospital.
This water glass with your lip-
and fingerprints. These relics which compose
a litany of artifacts seeking reassembly.

In the archives, shadows understand disappearance.
This is an exercise *in memoriam*
or some obfuscated recollection
of something inscribed elsewhere
and to die is different than any one supposed
and I imagine it as shutting off a light
and becoming darkness or turning on a light
and disappearing into the supernova
of the machine's flattered heart.

Tracking sites

Tracking sites I

[above]

above the uppermost   above pleas of saints   above whispers ricocheting   above the ionosphere   above the exosphere past dawnish haze   above several hundred miles   above earth   above fading light   above the conflict below   above supplication   above suspicion   above cirrostrati   over / beyond / upon   above freshly turned soil   above tree crowns rustled by wind   above obscenely streaking contrails

[*between*]

between source and recipient   between launch and strike   between utterance and echo   between flight and gravity

between pleas of saints and sound   between pleas to saints carried into space   between mnemonics and recall   between

gaps filled by reflections   between silence and song   amid / amidst / among   betwixt conceptions and

unremembered melodies   between tongue and lips   between the archives and forgetting   between *be* and *two each*

[*below*]

below the acme   below apex / apogee / the father / the sun   below the summit staring wistfully   below
upward   below ideas that prevent flight   below the vertex of flight   below the range of apex to zenith   below
the weight of begging   below supplication   below underlying desire under *desire*   below trinitite's blue-green
pane   below sand   past the nickel core of earth   below the earth's pedestal of turtle or crocodile back   below gravity

Tracking sites II

[within]

within the grip the chasm   within the grip is space to consider   within hidden cities   within innumerable houses innumerable lives within   within confines   within the brain   within the charred but barely known   within throat and chest   within each utterance   within billions of synapses   within infinite combinations   within the jagged science   within an embryo feeding from within   within the *I*   within atoms is movement   within movement   within the visible spectrum

82

[*with*]

with *ad infinitum*   with symmetry comes expectation   with the onset of winter light becomes bluer   with equinox
comes equilibrium   with constant monitoring   with boundaries   with the exception of out and in   with three
there is divinity   with synchronicity   with simultaneity   with a breakdown of memory   with each action there is
an equal and opposite reaction   with each action there is an equal   with each action there is   with each reaction

83

[*without*]

without summer's yellow light   without focus   without is   without minus / cipher / ought / naught / nil   without the burden of symmetry   without flattened affect   without the wish for   without reaction there is stasis   without light   without history or expectation   without boundaries   without response   without memory   without memory the past is *not*   without *not* no *is*   without death there is no commerce   without I   without center and motive   without a point on which to focus   without action   without world   without end

84

Tracking sites III

[before]

before forgetting and fatigue   before eras epochs and periods   before zero   before phosphenes obstruct sight   before hormones release   before clothes are shed   before anticipation   before the smell of bread   before the accretion of substrata   before fire-trails and cartoonish explosions   before red / orange / yellow   before antagonism and contraciction   before malice   before mummification   before priests catalog organs   before the parable of the corpse there is the corpse   before the indices   before this is recorded and stored   before effect   before precedents   before cause

[*during*]

during the continuous present   during the practice of forgetting   during the salt-packing of the body   during self-preservation and the practice of continuity   during the composition of parables   during paring down of facts   during the accumulation of fossil records   during fossil records in strata   during caresses and whispers   during meanwhile   during the interim   during the wearing down of molars   during the cataloguing of parts   during subduction   during green

[*after*]

ently / thereafter   postmeridian   after there   after the cause   aftereffect   aftermath   afterwards   after words   after memory   after blue   after indigo   after elapsed time   after duration   after the archives are forgotten   after the archives fall into disrepair   after records are scattered and declared relics of the old world   after the new world   after manuscripts fade and crumble   after violet what is there   after the graves   after their discovery   after flesh   after nude   after ~   after ~   after ~   after ~   after temporary repetition aphasia

87

Archived imperatives

Archived imperatives I

(A) I will show you where to stand
but the rooms are oblivious—the walls
the chair gently rocking itself
—to camouflage / *to disguise* / to hide among
sunrises—this is when we depart or
concede to *terra firma* duped by gravity or
baited by the seductive tuck of a bed
—the startling realness of some firm ground
when you expel one breath
in the name of exchange
withhold the other
in a game called survival
and do not share the spasms
that interfere with sleep

(B) Euphemize *mystery* as *terra incognita*

—an afflicted region / a stigmatized tract of shoulder

of shadow defining muscle

—a tract of land and water

tattooed on your stomach: *corpus incognito*

—as you pace the house vertical blinds cast striae

and accentuate your body's contours

—as you dictate your will indwelling

on the inception of light-ribbons

into every corner—we attempt momentary forays

into confusion to refute

what precedes future / what hinders us

what is hidden in the archives

(C) When walls sweat and buckle and

breathe / when air crackles with

staticky danger / when branch-heaps shelter rabbits

who leave misleading trails in widening spirals

—after a phoenix egg is conflagration and

the television's vertical shift

means more than it should

and when trumpet vines finally overwhelm

the awnings—then intestate but smiling

we can end and begin here

Archived imperatives II

(A) As soon as after-images ditto
away only negatives remain
discordant to sight and measure
—then only an irritation / a flicker
and beginning anew with atoms stripped
to lambent nothings / infinitesimal hums
revealed as corneal shadows
light whispers / baleful quivering flames—
thus the future transmutes and becomes
sexier with possibilities

(B) Imagine skull-windows / imagine evenings spent
in darkened rooms watching
synaptic exequies fire static / imagine the sun-
burst of arousal / supernovae of orgasms
fingers drawn along a thigh and imagine
fireworks—the terminal moment
when the brain gutters and sighs

(C) Enshadowed in song this morning
curled in a down comforter hair mussed
the duration of love-dreams / waking to
a lover's spider-web caress—comparable to sleep
to your eye-torqued decline
our crepuscular tongues salute morning and we reluct
to mourn the aftermath of musky sweat torn
between dusk / day / declension of night
the steadily dissolving ligatures between
an after-image / a flash-burn *trompe l'oeil*

Archived Imperatives III

(A) The stubborn flesh under-
finger the skin of your wrist reveals assailable veins
—called instinct to proceed / called
a gift to us among struggles—struggle
to breathe / struggle to remain tangled
in sheets / to penetrate the confines
of our bodies and the archives—the impulse
frightens us / to embellish
to mention parts / to disembody the body's
outlets and inlets and branches
and belly-curves—to articulate
these self-made mazes

(B) The diagrams of us are well lit
and parodic and blinds bind the house
inside / tree branches scrim windows
outside and the moon is awake and casts
shadows across carpet—it is still
not morning and you notice
the diminishment of fire-flies—
the loss in bursts / in increments
of lack-of-light and the unendurable progression
of a hand from spine to buttocks to thigh
—the models of you are uneasy and
esurient in their need to mimic

(C) But between us and the next
room dialectics are circular—
out of necessity labyrinthine and
what came first—my body / your *body*
our bodies fragile in abandonment
so vulnerable whether sky- or earth-obliged
in flight or take-off or a phoenix
emanating from its ashen domain—an ascension
that overwhelms the afternoon sun

Archived Imperatives IV

(A) Forty caresses a minute
is the ideal rhythm at dawn
but who needs an equation
to discover what happens when
our hands meet / when movement is feverish
mimicry / is reversal / is a cat's cradle
making a loop again / are drawings as rumors
—attend to your distrait yet well-lit
interior—your fingers measure
pulse / the insouciant pressure to measure
the extent of sunlight's
light years traveled

(B) This time-lapse photo I call
sleep / this future moribund and lock-stepped
in its progression—distraction leads to a loss
of space / of duration / of a hand that mines
darkness and warmth—unfailed to be moved
by lying bare back to back—anticipated collisions
of bodies are telegraphed from the interior
of bodies—to treat the subject requires
volumes / requires music unrehearsed
and cordant—no *dis*- because
this must be melodious

(C) Amazed and obviated we lie side
by side—eyes scopic / panoptic—
huddled with indurate light cupped
in palms—a fairy-light / an infant
cradled in an elbow's crook
cries to remain unpreyed-upon / to remind
us to breathe—your hands / these hands / our hands
their provenances questionable—
searching—gradations too subtle / recall
too slow and a disappearance—we can press
our eyelids to conjure red lightning and our brains
flash—so many presents to come

Temporal versions

Temporal versions

0. This lode around which day-pieces accrete smacks of shard
and collage, macaronic hodge-podge and cognates—words attracted
to almost-faces and people-not-exactly. How filings radiate ferrous spines
around magnets or how ova and spermatozoa attract or when a sea-urchin
cracked reveals embryonic orange, fetal-curled in its echinate pod.

1. An ambush sets mouths in motion. Demands set the world
in motion—which does revolve around you, the now-axis
and when you close your eyes the world does disappear.
This magic is snake-oil, these archives sleight-of-hand. You are closer
than you appear in the mirror. Dreams are not magic and do not restrain dawn.
Nights shorten and every day has its temporal sinkholes.

2. Autumn slinks into color and absence and part of me
believes fallen leaves laugh relieved and stare up at canopy gaps
unwilling or just unable to hide over-wintering birds.
Absence tears swatches from memories not yet petrified
in memory. Drawn in breezy slashes, wood smoke points
geese southward leaving caesurae for another season.

3. Cut to utterance guttural is literal but misunderstood entirely.
Noise: shadows of words that tremble in dreams.
Night: time to wonder when the din will cease or if it can.
Intruding upon sleep, dreams are day-piece mosaics
of city-wandering, of not-quite-tragedies, too many almost-loves
and footfalls to count, sorted, reconstituted in outbursts.

4. Every harmony evanesces into monotony, adjourns under
the weight of tedium. Faded anthems and marches.
A nagging sensation of something that only feels final.
One finger cannot fetter a cracked dam. You need new
words for aural phantoms, to consider the echo, to consider
limbic impulses that guide your hands to my lips.
Listen: this is why we must speak:

5. What I know is mostly mosaic—more missing than there—
recreated in dark hours and providing sound advice: proceed
with caution across the fractured landscape you navigate.
Tonight is shadows cast by today. Outside—past curtain and window
—rain tamps fallen leaves. First a sharp rapping, shade sounds,
then soft lullaby drum taps, waking words uncertain in my mouth.

6. There is so much to say before water rushes to cover
us. This is why, according to its clerks, every era is most
infernal. The echo's origin is curséd. Some sounds
too unbearable to hear twice. Stolen refrains called history.
You threw your last *sabot* into the resolute machines. You cannot
reclaim a coin tossed into a pond—it fluttered to the bottom
years ago, a spark awaiting fingers to snatch it from murk.

7. Breathe and die—hard to discern any difference as soil
disintegrates into more useful molecules, more necessary iotas.
In loamy dank micro-organisms multiply. Tulip bulbs stockpile sun
and sugars to spear soil cast over them, to see the *sol* denied.
Their desire for revenge may be my desire to believe they care—
that they harbor resentment, that they dream of beaches several and temperate.

8. God-machines groan and unreel films of a needle drawn
through gauze. A needle drawn through gauze. Time-lapse sequences
uneasy arrangements made with seasons, austere trees
italicized by wind. Part of me believes daylight will return
from behind whatever curtain adumbrates it. Another part of me calls
this hope—nothing hearkened with trumpet blasts—just diminutive
sighs rising from neighbors' chimneys, their exhaustion apparent, forgivable,

Acknowledgements

Much gratitude to the editors of the following journals in which most of these poems first appeared (sometimes in slightly different forms):

26	"Temporal versions 0.", "Temporal versions 1.", "Temporal versions 2.", "Temporal versions 3.", "Temporal versions 4.", "Temporal versions 5.", "Temporal versions 6.", "Temporal versions 7.", "Temporal versions 8."
Barrow Street	"Abbreviated inventories I (C)"
Colorado Review	"Breath variations 5.", "Breath variations 6.", "Breath variations 7.", "Breath variations 8.", "Breath variations 9."
Cricket Online Review	"Catalogued evidence 0.", "Catalogued evidence 1.", "Catalogued evidence 2.", "Catalogued evidence 3.", "Catalogued evidence 4.", "Catalogued evidence 5.", "Catalogued evidence 6.", "Catalogued evidence 7.", "Catalogued evidence 8.", "Catalogued evidence 9.", "Catalogued evidence 10.", "Catalogued evidence 11.", "Catalogued evidence 12.", "Catalogued evidence 13."
DoubleRoom	"Translation briefs 0:", "Translation briefs 1:", "Translation briefs 2:", "Translation briefs 3:", "Translation briefs 4:", "Translation briefs 5:", "Translation briefs 6:", "Translation briefs 7:", "Translation briefs 8:", "Translation briefs 9:"

Five Fingers Review	"Abbreviated inventories II (A)",
	"Abbreviated inventories II (B)",
	"Abbreviated inventories II (C)"
Hunger Magazine	"Archived imperatives I (A)",
	"Archived imperatives I (B)",
	"Archived imperatives I (C)"
Interim	"Abbreviated inventories IV (A)",
	"Abbreviated inventories IV (B)",
	"Abbreviated inventories IV (C)"
Isotope	"Tracking sites I [*above*]",
	"Tracking sites I [*between*]",
	"Tracking sites I [*below*]"
Laurel Review	"Archived imperatives III (A)",
	"Archived imperatives III (B)",
	"Archived imperatives III (C)"
*Western Humanities Review	"Abbreviated inventories III (A)",
	"Abbreviated inventories III (B)",
	"Abbreviated inventories III (C)",
	"Abbreviated inventories V (A)",
	"Abbreviated inventories V (B)",
	"Abbreviated inventories V (C)"

*These poems were selected as finalists by Mary Jo Bang for the 2004 Utah Writers Competition.

As always, infinite love and thanks to Jacqueline Lyons—The Lilac Thief—partner and reader extraordinaire.

To Donald Revell and Claudia Keelan for their continual inspiration and friendship.

To Rusty Morrison and Ken Keegan for their clarity of sight.

To Joshua Kryah and Matthew Cooperman for their keen critiques.

And of course: Peter Covino, Ryan Hoglund, and c.a. liebow—partners in crime and beyond.

Christopher Arigo's first poetry collection *Lit interim* won the 2001-2002 Transcontinental Poetry Prize (selected by David Bromige) and was published by Pavement Saw Press. Currently a Schaeffer Poetry Fellow at the University of Nevada, Las Vegas, he is also the Managing Editor of the literary magazine *Interim*.